Rain Forests
INSIDE OUT

Robin Johnson

CRABTREE
Publishing Company
www.crabtreebooks.com

Author: Robin Johnson
**Publishing plan research
 and series development:** Reagan Miller
Editorial director: Kathy Middleton
Editors: Sarah Eason, Jennifer Sanderson,
 Nancy Dickmann, and Shirley Duke
Proofreader: Wendy Scavuzzo
Project coordinator: Sarah Eason
Design: Paul Myerscough
Photo research: Rachel Blount
**Production coordinator and
 Prepress technician:** Tammy McGarr
Print coordinator: Katherine Berti

Written, developed, and produced by Calcium

Photo Credits:

t=Top, bl=Bottom Left, br=Bottom Right

Corbis: Wim Klomp/Foto Natura/Minden Pictures: p. 11 (tr):
Dreamstime: Barbara Helgason: p. 16–17; Pavol Kmeto: p. 8–9; Chris
Moncrieff: p. 1 (br), p. 19 (br); Tzooka: p. 14–15; Peter Wollinga:
p. 4–5; Leszek Wrona: p. 22–23: Shutterstock: Anton_Ivanov: p. 9 (br);
Hagit Berkovich: p. 11 (tr); Gualtiero Boffi: p. 3; Chainfoto24: p. 12–13;
CrackerClips Stock Media: p. 6–7; Timothy Epp: p. 25 (tr); Dirk Ercken:
p. 17 (tr); Fotomicar: p. 27 (br); Filipe Frazao: p. 20–21; GWImages:
p. 29 (b); Pablo Hidalgo: p. 28–29; Lightpoet: p. 28; MarcusVDT: p. 13
(br); Dr. Morley Read: p. 1, p. 18–19; Szefei: p. 10–11; Rob van Esch:
p. 24–25; Worldswildlifewonders: p. 15 (tr); Feng Yu: p. 26–27: Wikimedia
Commons: Hollingsworth, John and Karen/U.S. Fish & Wildlife Service:
p. 23 (br).

Cover: Dreamstime: Ingvars; John Caezar Panelo (br).

Library and Archives Canada Cataloguing in Publication

Johnson, Robin (Robin R.), author
 Rain forests inside out / Robin Johnson.

(Ecosystems inside out)
Includes index.
Issued in print and electronic formats.
ISBN 978-0-7787-0637-3 (bound).--
ISBN 978-0-7787-1458-3 (pbk.).--
ISBN 978-1-4271-7649-3 (pdf).--ISBN 978-1-4271-7643-1 (html)

 1. Rain forest ecology--Juvenile literature. 2. Rain forest
animals--Juvenile literature. I. Title.

QH541.5.R27J64 2014   j577.34   C2014-903763-5
                                        C2014-903764-3

Library of Congress Cataloging-in-Publication Data

Johnson, Robin (Robin R.)
 Rain forests inside out / Robin Johnson.
  pages cm. -- (Ecosystems inside out)
 Includes index.
 ISBN 978-0-7787-0637-3 (reinforced library binding) --
ISBN 978-0-7787-1458-3 (pbk.) --
ISBN 978-1-4271-7649-3 (electronic pdf) --
ISBN 978-1-4271-7643-1 (electronic html)
1. Rain forest ecology--Juvenile literature. 2. Rain forests--
Juvenile literature. I. Title.

QH541.5.R27.J67 2015
577.34--dc23

                                        2014020968

Crabtree Publishing Company
www.crabtreebooks.com   1-800-387-7650

Printed in the U.S.A./022015/CG20150122

Published in Canada
Crabtree Publishing
616 Welland Ave.
St. Catharines, Ontario
L2M 5V6

Published in the United States
Crabtree Publishing
PMB 59051
350 Fifth Avenue, 59th Floor
New York, New York 10118

Published in the United Kingdom
Crabtree Publishing
Maritime House
Basin Road North, Hove
BN41 1WR

Published in Australia
Crabtree Publishing
3 Charles Street
Coburg North
VIC, 3058

Contents

What Is an Ecosystem?

An **ecosystem** is made up of **organisms**, the environment in which they live, and their **interrelationships**. Each living thing in an ecosystem depends on other living and nonliving things for its survival. Living things are called **biotic factors**. Nonliving things, such as sunlight, water, and soil, are called **abiotic factors**. A healthy ecosystem has great **biodiversity**, meaning many **species**, or types, of plants and animals live there. Their needs are met by the biotic and abiotic factors in their ecosystem.

All Shapes and Sizes

Ecosystems can be large or small. An entire ecosystem can be found in a single tree trunk! A **biome** is a large geographical area that contains similar plants, animals, and environments. Rain forests, oceans, wetlands, grasslands, tundras, and deserts are some of Earth's biomes.

What Are Rain Forests?

Rain forests are thick, **lush** forests that get at least 80 inches (203 cm) of rain each year. When you think of rain forests, you probably picture colorful **tropical** rain forests in South America and other hot places. Did you know there are also rain forests in North America? **Temperate** rain forests are found along coasts in places that have warm summers and cool winters.

Grab an umbrella and let's explore the highs and lows of rain forest ecosystems! We'll look at each ecosystem as a whole, then explore one branch of it further.

What Is a System?

A **system** is a group of separate parts that work together for a purpose. The parts of ecosystems are plants, animals, water, oxygen, and other biotic and abiotic factors. The right amount of abiotic factors in an ecosystem help maintain the biotic factors as they interact. Each part of an ecosystem has a specific and important role that helps the ecosystem function. Ecosystems work in a delicate balance, however. A change to just one part of an ecosystem can affect all the other parts of the ecosystem.

Key

- Deserts
- Grasslands
- Oceans
- Rain forests
- Tundras
- Wetlands

This map shows where rain forests and other biomes are found around the world.

Rain forests depend on water, sunlight, soil, and other abiotic factors for their survival.

Energy in Ecosystems

sun

From the tiniest butterfly to the tallest tree, every living thing in a rain forest ecosystem needs **energy** to survive. Energy comes from food. A **food chain** shows how an organism gets energy from food, and how it is then passed from one organism to another. Many different organisms rely on one food chain.

Plants Make Food

Plants are called producers because they make their own food through **photosynthesis**. Photosynthesis is a process in which plants use chlorophyll in their leaves and sunlight to change carbon dioxide and water into food and oxygen.

Animals are consumers. They must eat food to get the energy they need. Primary consumers are animals that eat plants. They are also called herbivores. Secondary consumers are meat-eaters that consume other animals for food. They are also called carnivores. Omnivores eat both plants and animals.

Decomposers are organisms that break down dead plant and animal matter. They put back **nutrients** into the soil. Plants use the nutrients to grow and the food chain begins again.

World Wide Webs

Every living thing in a rain forest is connected to other living things in the rain forest. When energy flows between organisms in different food chains, it creates a **food web**. Healthy food webs are made up of many plant and animal species whose needs are met in the web.

Astrocaryum fruit tree → **howler monkey** → **harpy eagle**

This food chain shows the flow of energy from one organism to another.

Trees and other plants are at the bottom of all rain forest food chains. They make food that animals in rain forest ecosystems need to survive.

Eco Up Close

All living things need water, and rain forests get plenty of it! It rains onto the trees and drips all the way down to their roots. Rain is a form of **precipitation**. It is part of the water cycle that keeps water moving around Earth. The other parts of the water cycle are **evaporation** and **condensation**. All rain forest ecosystems need unpolluted, or clean, water to stay healthy.

Rain or Shine

Rain forests are divided into four layers. From treetop to the ground, they are the emergent layer, the canopy, the understory, and the forest floor. Each layer gets a different amount of sunlight, wind, and water. Different plants and animals have **adapted** to the abiotic factors in each layer. To adapt is to change over a long period of time or many generations to better survive an environment.

Life in the Layers

The emergent layer towers high above the forest floor. The sun is hot and the wind is strong there, so only **hardy** species can survive. The few animals that live there—such as birds and bats—must be skilled fliers or climbers to find food and stay safe.

The **dense** canopy gets plenty of water and sunlight, but it is protected from strong winds and heat, so most tropical plants and animals live in this busy layer. There is a lot of **prey** for **predators** to catch and eat in the canopy.

The understory is cool and shady. Some plants have adapted to grow in this dim layer, while others climb from the understory to the canopy to reach sunlight. Frogs, snakes, lizards, and many other animals make their homes there.

Few plants live on the dark floor of tropical rain forests, but the biggest and smallest animals are found there. Large cats and other predators hunt for prey in this layer. **Microscopic** decomposers break down dead plants and animals that fall to the ground.

From the emergent treetops down to the forest floor, each layer is important to rain forest ecosystems.

understory

forest floor

emergent layer

canopy

Eco Up Close

Howler monkeys are large, slow-moving monkeys that are well suited to life in the canopy of tropical rain forests. They are herbivores that eat the leaves of trees. They make very loud howling sounds that allow them to communicate with other faraway howler monkeys without having to travel through the dense forest.

howler monkey

Tropical Rain Forests

Tropical rain forests are lush **broadleaf** forests found near the equator in South America, Central America, Africa, southeast Asia, and Australia. The **climate** in tropical rain forests is warm and wet. Temperatures range from 68 to 93 degrees Fahrenheit (20 to 34 °C) all year. There is plenty of sunlight and it rains most days. With so much sunlight and water, many plants can grow. A forest full of plants provides food for the many animals living there.

Jewels of the Earth

Tropical rain forests cover only about six percent of Earth's surface, but they are home to more than half the plant and animal species in the world! There is more biodiversity in rain forests than in any other biome on Earth. Rain forest plants make oxygen that all living things in the forest—and around the world— need to survive. Animals take in oxygen and release carbon dioxide back into the air. Plants use the carbon dioxide to make food and more oxygen. Like all living things in ecosystems, rain forest plants and animals are **interdependent**. Interdependent organisms rely on one another for their survival.

Tropical rain forests are called the "jewels of the Earth." They are filled with rare and precious species.

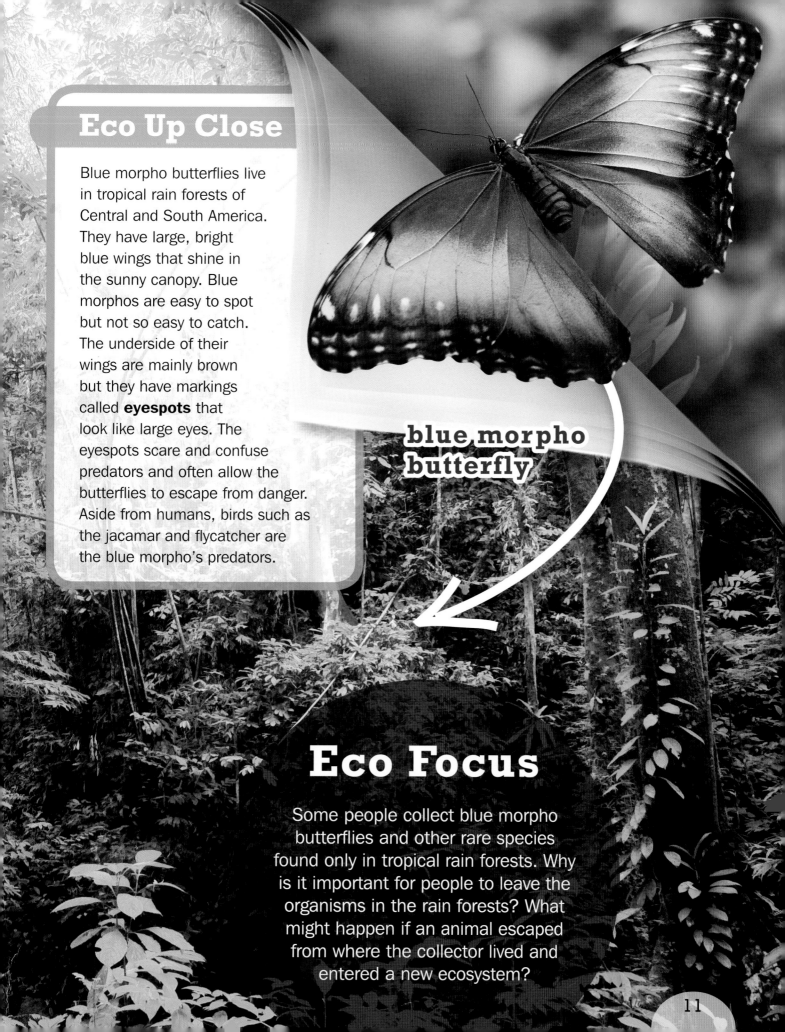

Eco Up Close

Blue morpho butterflies live in tropical rain forests of Central and South America. They have large, bright blue wings that shine in the sunny canopy. Blue morphos are easy to spot but not so easy to catch. The underside of their wings are mainly brown but they have markings called **eyespots** that look like large eyes. The eyespots scare and confuse predators and often allow the butterflies to escape from danger. Aside from humans, birds such as the jacamar and flycatcher are the blue morpho's predators.

blue morpho butterfly

Eco Focus

Some people collect blue morpho butterflies and other rare species found only in tropical rain forests. Why is it important for people to leave the organisms in the rain forests? What might happen if an animal escaped from where the collector lived and entered a new ecosystem?

Life on Top

The emergent layer of a tropical rain forest is made up of huge, mushroom-shaped trees that poke through the canopy. Some trees grow up to 250 feet (76 m) tall! There is no shade or shelter high in the sky. The sun blazes, temperatures soar, the rain beats down, and the wind blows hard. Life on top is tough, but some plants and animals have adapted to survive in this harsh **habitat**.

The tallest and toughest trees are found in the emergent layer of the rain forest.

Treetop Animals

Birds, bats, and insects make their homes in the emergent layer. They fly down into the canopy to find food, then return to their treetop habitats. These animals are important to the ecosystem because they help **pollinate** rain forest plants. To pollinate is to spread pollen, a fine powdery substance that plants need to make seeds and **reproduce**. Animals get pollen on their bodies when they feed on fruit and flowers. They carry the pollen with them as they fly, and it brushes off when they land on other plants.

Hardy Plants

Trees that grow in the emergent layer have small, waxy leaves that can stand up to the hot sun and strong winds. Many trees have light, fluffy seeds or seeds with "wings" that are easily spread by the wind. The towering kapok tree has foul-smelling flowers that attract fruit bats. The bats drink **nectar** from the flowers and help pollinate the plants in the process.

Eco Up Close

Harpy eagles are **apex predators** that live in the emergent layer. Apex predators are animals at the top of the food chain that have few or no natural predators. Harpy eagles are built for hunting. They have large, powerful wings and talons, or claws. They also have excellent vision and hearing. Harpy eagles perch on high branches and search for sloths, monkeys, and other animals in the canopy below. They dive through the leaves, grab their prey with their strong talons, and return to their treetop nests to feed.

harpy eagle

In the Canopy

The canopy is the treetop home of most rain forest plants and animals. Most trees in this active layer reach 60 to 130 feet (18 to 39 m) above the ground. Their long branches and lush green leaves form a huge umbrella over the forest. The canopy gets a lot of sunlight and water, so many types of plants grow there. Most have leaves with long, narrow ends called drip tips. Drip tips allow extra water to run off the leaves so that the plants stay dry and healthy.

Spreading Seeds

Since there is little wind in the canopy, plants rely on animals to pollinate them and spread their seeds. Many tropical plants have brightly colored or strong-smelling flowers that attract animals to them. Others grow tasty fruits that have seeds inside. Animals eat the fruit and spread the seeds in their waste.

Arboreal Animals

The canopy is home to birds, monkeys, sloths, snakes, lizards, insects, and many other animals. Several of these animals find food, shelter, and **mates** without ever coming down to the ground. These **arboreal**, or tree-dwelling, animals have adapted to life in the trees. For example, some monkeys have strong **prehensile** tails for holding or hanging from tree branches. Toucans have long beaks to get fruit on hard-to-reach branches. Tree kangaroos have short, broad feet that grip the trees, and long tails for balance.

three-toed sloth

More than one quarter of the world's bird species, including this toucan, live in tropical rain forests.

Eco Up Close

Three-toed sloths are large herbivores that hang around in the canopy. They eat mainly leaves, which do not give them much energy. Sloths move very slowly to **conserve**, or save, energy and to avoid being seen by predators. Sloths have a **mutualistic relationship** with the bacteria that live on their fur. The sloths give these tiny, single-celled organisms a sheltered home in the canopy. In return, the green bacteria cover the sloths' fur, helping them hide among the leaves.

In the Understory

The understory is the cool, shady part of the rain forest between the leafy treetops and the ground below. The dense canopy blocks most of the sunlight from reaching this part of the forest, so only plants that have adapted to grow in low light can survive there.

Growing in the Shade

Shrubs, palms, and woody plants grow well in the dim understory. Many of these plants have large leaves to absorb as much sunlight as possible. Other plants, such as the woody liana vines, have roots in the soil but climb tall trees to reach sunlight. Some plants are not rooted in the earth. Ferns, orchids, and bromeliads are **epiphytes**, or plants that grow on other plants but are not parasites. They sprout on branches and tree trunks in the understory and use them for support.

Undercover in the Understory

The understory is sheltered from high temperatures, heavy rains, and strong winds. So many animals, such as birds, snakes, tree frogs, lizards, jaguars, leopards, and insects, make their homes there. There is plenty of prey for predators to catch—if they can find it! Many animals in the understory and other parts of the rain forest are **camouflaged**. They have colors or markings that help them blend in with their surroundings and hide from predators. However, camouflage also helps predators, such as emerald tree boas and clouded leopards, hide and surprise their prey!

Emerald tree boas surprise their prey and squeeze the animals to death.

Eco Up Close

Red-eyed tree frogs are **amphibians** that live in the understory. They have sticky pads on their toes for climbing up and down trees, and strong legs for jumping from branch to branch. These little frogs count on camouflage to hide them from birds, bats, and snakes. Other amphibians, such as poison dart frogs, have brightly colored bodies that warn predators that it is dangerous to eat them.

red-eyed tree frog

The Forest Floor

The forest floor is a dark, **humid** area at the bottom of a tropical rain forest. The soil is shallow and does not contain many nutrients. They have been washed away by heavy rains over time. Thick trees block almost all the sunlight from this part of the forest, so few plants can grow there. The canopy's tall trees are rooted in the forest floor, however. Since trees cannot grow deep roots in the shallow soil, they form **buttress roots** instead. Buttress roots are huge, shallow roots that surround tall trees and keep them from falling over. The roots also spread out around the trees and help them reach nutrients in the soil.

Dining on Detritus

Since the soil is poor, most plants get the nutrients they need from **detritus**. Detritus is decaying plant and animal matter. Leaves, branches, seeds, fruits, and dead animals fall from the top layers of the rain forest to the floor below. **Scavengers**, such as snails, termites, and worms, eat the remains of dead animals they find. They break down the waste into small bits that bacteria, **fungi**, and other microscopic decomposers eat. The decomposers add important nutrients to the soil that plants need to grow.

Buttress roots spread out from tall trees in all directions to reach nutrients in the shallow soil.

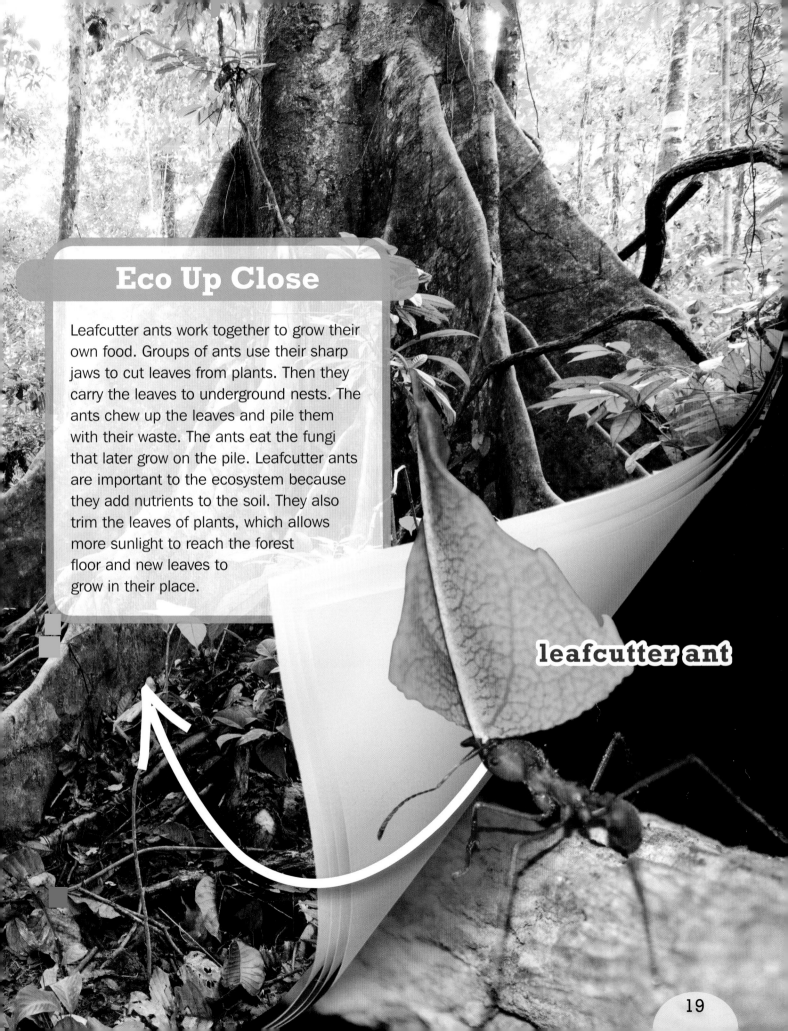

Eco Up Close

Leafcutter ants work together to grow their own food. Groups of ants use their sharp jaws to cut leaves from plants. Then they carry the leaves to underground nests. The ants chew up the leaves and pile them with their waste. The ants eat the fungi that later grow on the pile. Leafcutter ants are important to the ecosystem because they add nutrients to the soil. They also trim the leaves of plants, which allows more sunlight to reach the forest floor and new leaves to grow in their place.

leafcutter ant

The Amazing Amazon

The Amazon rain forest is the biggest, busiest, and most biodiverse rain forest in the world. It covers a whopping 3 to 3.2 million square miles (7.76 to 8.29 million sq km) of land! More than two thirds of the rain forest is found in Brazil. Parts of the rain forest are also found in Peru, Colombia, Venezuela, and other countries in South America. Like all rain forests, the Amazon rain forest gets a large amount of precipitation. The rain feeds the mighty Amazon River and many other rivers that flow through the forest.

Species in Danger

From the tallest trees to the darkest forest floor, the Amazon rain forest is full of life. One out of every ten known species lives there! Scarlet macaws squawk in the treetops. Active squirrel monkeys climb and leap from branch to branch. Huge anacondas and little piranhas search for prey in the water.

Many of the Amazon rain forest species are **endangered**. People cut down millions of trees in the Amazon and other rain forests each year. They clear the forests to build homes, farms, mines, and roads. Without their rain forest habitats, the plants and animals have nowhere to live. Their **populations** shrink and the entire ecosystem suffers.

Eco Focus

One fifth of the Amazon rain forest has already been destroyed. What do you think will happen to the plants and animals that live there if people keep cutting down the trees?

There are millions of plant and animal species in the Amazon rain forest.

Eco Up Close

Black caimans are large **crocodilians** that live in rivers in the Amazon rain forest. They are strong, swift hunters that use their sharp teeth to grab prey in the water or on the riverbank. They drown their prey before eating it. Black caimans eat fish, anacondas, monkeys, tapirs, capybaras, and any other prey they find. They are a **keystone species** in the Amazon ecosystem because they help control the populations of many animals.

black caiman

Temperate Rain Forests

Temperate rain forests are rare, very old forests of giant trees. They are found along the coasts of oceans between the tropics and polar regions. The largest area of temperate rain forest stretches from Alaska to northern California on the west coast of North America. There are also temperate rain forests in Chile, the United Kingdom, New Zealand, Australia, and a few other parts of the world.

Foggy Forests

The climate in temperate rain forests is mild and wet. Temperatures range from 50 to 75 degrees Fahrenheit (10 to 24 °C) all year. Temperate rain forests receive less rain than tropical rain forests do, but they get plenty of **moisture** from fog. Fog is thick clouds made up of tiny water droplets that float near the surface of Earth. Fog rolls in off the ocean and drifts into temperate rain forests. It coats the leaves of the trees with moisture. Some of the water drips down to the ground as precipitation.

A Canopy of Conifers

The trees in temperate rain forests are mostly **conifers**. Conifers are trees that have cones and needlelike leaves. The wet conditions of these forests cause some conifers to grow tall with a thick trunk. Species such as Douglas fir, Sitka spruce, and western hemlock tower over the forest floor. Some trees are hundreds of years old and more than 300 feet (91 m) high! These **old-growth forests** may keep growing and growing unless they are affected by fires, windstorms, or people who cut down the trees.

Eco Focus

Old-growth forests are cut down by the **logging industry** to make lumber and paper. What actions can you take to conserve the rain forest resources and save trees to help keep this ecosystem in balance? Explain your ideas.

Giant old-growth trees tower over the floor of temperate rain forests.

Eco Up Close

Northern spotted owls nest in old-growth forests on the west coast of North America. They are carnivores that hunt wood rats and flying squirrels over large areas of the forests. The owls are endangered because people are destroying their habitats.

northern spotted owl

Under the Conifers

Giant conifers are not the only plants that grow in temperate rain forests. The abiotic conditions are ideal for many other species, too. The canopy is not as dense as in tropical rain forests, so more sunlight reaches the forest floor. The soil is thicker and richer in nutrients than in tropical rain forests. It has not been washed away by the heavy rains that hit tropical lands. There are also fewer species of trees in temperate forests, so there is less competition among plants for nutrients.

Made for Shade

Small broadleaf trees, such as vine maples and Pacific dogwoods, grow well in the understory. Salmonberry, huckleberry, and other shrubs are also common. Wildflowers, grasses, and small plants cover the forest floor. Other plants, such as **mosses**, **lichens**, and ferns, are epiphytes. They grow all over the trunks and branches of conifers in search of sunlight.

If a Tree Falls in the Forest

When a huge conifer falls in the forest, it can take hundreds of years for fungi, insects, and other decomposers to break it down. While it is decaying, the dead tree is called a **nurse log**. It gives plants important nutrients and a safe place to sprout and grow. It also provides a habitat for small animals. Nurse logs are an example of **commensalism** in a rain forest ecosystem. Commensalism is a relationship between two organisms in which one benefits and the other is not affected.

Temperate rain forests are green machines! The abiotic conditions of these forests allow many plants to grow, covering the forest floor.

redwood sorrel

Eco Up Close

The redwood sorrel is a short flowering plant found in temperate rain forests in North America. It has heart-shaped leaves and grows well on the shady forest floor. The redwood sorrel has adapted to carry out photosynthesis in very low light. In fact, too much light can damage the plant! Its leaves fold downward in direct sunlight to protect it from harm.

Food on the Floor

There are plenty of plants in temperate rain forests, so many animals live there. Most animals make their homes on or near the temperate rain forest floor, where they are sheltered from the rain, wind, and sun. Primary consumers search for plant foods on the ground. Birds, squirrels, chipmunks, deer, elk, and many other herbivores find seeds, berries, mushrooms, grass, leaves, and cones to eat. Mule deer feed on conifers. They are one of the few species that have adapted to eat the prickly needles and sharp twigs on the trees.

Plenty of Prey

Secondary consumers find an **abundance** of prey in temperate rain forests. Small predators such as woodpeckers and frogs, catch insects. Larger predators, such as owls, raccoons, and weasels, eat smaller predators. Bears, wolves, and cougars, the apex predators, eat deer, elk, and other large prey they hunt on the forest floor.

Many predators catch salmon in the ocean and in rivers that flow through temperate rain forests. Salmon are a keystone species because they provide food for a wide variety of animals. They also bring energy and important nutrients from the ocean biome into the rain forest biome.

Grizzly bears are omnivores. They search the forest floor for plants and animals to eat. They are also scavengers that eat dead animals they find.

Eco Focus

Trophy hunters prize grizzly bears, cougars, and other large animals that live in temperate rain forests. Trophy hunters catch wild game animals for sport. Large predators are needed to control animal populations in rain forests. How could hunting these animals disrupt the balance of rain forest ecosystems?

Eco Up Close

Pudús are the smallest deer in the world. They grow no more than 18 inches (46 cm) tall! These deer live in temperate rain forests in South America. Pudú populations are small, too. They are endangered as a result of **overhunting** and habitat loss.

pudú

Rain Check

Rain forests are the jewels of the Earth. They provide a rich and colorful habitat for millions of species. They supply energy for animals up and down the food chain. The huge number of plants make oxygen that all living things need to survive. Rain forests also affect rain and weather patterns around the world. Precipitation falls in rain forests as part of the water cycle. Plants absorb some of the water through their roots. They also put moisture back into the air through their leaves. The wind carries the water to other places that need rain. We need rain forests—and rain forests need our help.

What Can You Do?

Use less paper. Billions of trees are cut down each year to make paper. If we use less paper, fewer trees will be destroyed.

Research which companies damage or destroy rain forests to make their products. Send them emails and tell them you refuse to buy what they sell.

Never buy monkeys, frogs, snakes, or other pets that come from tropical rain forests. They belong in their natural habitats.

Keep on reading and learning about rain forest ecosystems. Then spread the word and keep rain forests growing!

Activity:

Many of the foods we eat each day—
bananas, oranges, chocolate, vanilla,
sugar, and coffee—come from tropical
rain forests around the world. Your
mission is to follow the path
of one food item from
forest to fridge.

Instructions

1. Choose a food from the list in the box above or research
   other foods grown in tropical rain forests.
2. Then go online to learn about the food. For example:
   - Find out where the food was grown and show it on a map.
   - Discover how the food was farmed and processed.
     Was it harmful to the ecosystem?
   - Find out how the food got from the rain forest to the
     grocery store. Get on the trail and follow that food!

Glossary

Please note: Some bold-faced words are defined in the text

abiotic factors Nonliving parts of an ecosystem, such as water and soil

arboreal Living in trees

abundance A good or healthy supply

amphibians Animals such as frogs and salamanders that begin life in water, then live on land as adults

biodiversity The variety of plant and animal life in an ecosystem or other area on Earth

biotic factors Living parts of an ecosystem, such as plants and animals

broadleaf Describing trees or other plants with wide, flat leaves

camouflaged Colored or shaped to blend in with the surroundings

climate The normal weather in a specific area

condensation The process in which water vapor cools and changes to liquid form

conserve To save something, or in the case of materials such as paper, to use less of it

crocodilians Large reptiles with long, thin mouths, short legs, and powerful tails

dense Thick; having parts that are crowded closely together

ecosystem A group of living and nonliving things that live and interact in an area

endangered At risk of dying out

energy The power that nutrients from food provide to the body

epiphytes Plants that grow on other plants but are not parasites; for example, orchid plants grow on tree trunks

evaporation The process in which water is heated by the sun and changed from a liquid into a gas called water vapor

eyespots Eyelike markings on animals used to discourage predators by making the prey appear larger or more frightening

food chain A chain of organisms in which each member uses the member below as food

food web The interlinked food chains in an ecosystem

fungi Organisms that absorb food from their environment, such as mold

habitat The natural environment of an animal or plant

hardy Able to withstand harsh conditions

humid Damp; describing air that contains a large amount of water vapor

interrelationships The relationships between many different organisms and their environment

keystone species A species that plays such an important role in its environment that it affects many other organisms

lichens Types of organisms made up of fungi and algae living together in a mutualistic relationship

logging industry A group of businesses that cut down trees to use the wood to make goods such as paper or furniture

lush Covered with full, healthy, green plants

mates Partners that animals need so they can reproduce

microscopic So small that it can be seen only by using a microscope

moisture Wetness that can be felt in the air or seen as liquid on the surface of objects

mosses Small plants that grow on damp ground and do not have flowers or roots

mutualistic relationship A close relationship between two or more species that benefits or helps both species

nectar A sweet liquid found in some flowers

nurse log A large, fallen, and decaying tree trunk that provides moisture and nutrients for many insects and plants

nutrients Substances that allow organisms to thrive and grow

old-growth forests Forests that have grown for a long time without being damaged or logged

organisms Living things

overhunting Hunting too many of one species

pollinate To transfer pollen grains to the part of a plant that can reproduce

populations The total numbers of species in an area

precipitation Water that falls from the clouds as rain, snow, sleet, or hail

predators Animals that hunt other animals for food

prehensile Describing body parts that can grasp or hold objects

prey An animal that is hunted by another animal for food

reproduce To produce offspring

scavengers Animals that feed on the dead remains of other animals

species A group of animals or plants that are similar and can produce young

temperate A temperature that is not too hot, and not too cold

tropical Describing a hot and humid climate

Learning More

Find out more about Earth's precious rain forest ecosystems.

Books

Gazlay, Suzy. *Managing Green Spaces: Careers in Wilderness and Wildlife Management.* New York, NY: Crabtree Publishing Company, 2009.

Latham, Donna. *Endangered Biomes: Rain Forests.* Norwich, VT: Nomad Press, 2011.

Moore, Heidi. *Rain Forest Food Chains.* Mankato, MN: Heinemann Library, 2010.

Websites

You'll find facts, stories, activities, and games on this useful Rain forest Alliance site at:
www.rain forest-alliance.org/kids

This National Geographic website offers a collection of articles, photos, videos, and activities about rain forests:
http://education.nationalgeographic.com/education/topics/rain-forests/?ar_a=1

Follow this link to learn more about tropical and temperate rain forests, as well as other biomes and ecosystems around the world:
www.mbgnet.net/sets/rforest/index.htm

Visit this site to meet some rain forest heroes and learn how you can help, too!
http://rain forestheroes.ran.org/take-action-online

Index